DEFECTIVE DETECTIVES
NOTHING IS AS IT SEEMS

What's more dangerous than a top thief on the loose or a ton of missing jewellery or a fishy business deal? A pair of wannabe detectives trying to solve any of the above! Rahul and Ravi are the infamous Defective Detectives, who have vowed to solve every mystery on this planet. And if and when there is no mystery, rest assured they will invent one! You see, with their laudable imagination and unwavering determination, the duo are always hot on the heels of trouble or more often than not, trouble is hot on their heels! Either way, it is no mystery that absolute pandemonium is bound to follow when these two are aboard. So stick around close. It would be a crime to miss out on all the madness and mayhem that breaks loose in the world of the Defective Detectives!

Love you, Rahul and Ravi! Continue to mess up and be very sloppy!
– **Srinath Swaminathan**, Hyderabad

Defective Detectives' hilarious potboilers leave me laughing my head off!
– **Tanisha Bhatnagar**, Agra

Defective Detectives sharpen my detective skills to become Sherlock Holmes!
– **Deepali Gupta**, Mumbai

Rahul and Ravi motivate children to become detectives. Even I want to be a detective after reading their funny stories.
– **Chinmayee V.**

Defective Detectives, I love your clumsy adventures! I like your li'l sis, Sam, too, Ravi! I have a plan for you. If you don't want Sam to bother you, don't tell her where you're going! I hope that works.
– **S. Bhavishya**, Chennai

7

9

Defective Detectives and The MASTERMIND!

Story: Sharmistha Sinha
Script: R. Nalini
Art: Abhijeet Kini

SUNDAY MORNING AND OUR ACE DETECTIVES ARE ON AN IMPORTANT MISSION –

I'M ON THE LAST PAGE OF THE NOVEL... I'M GOING TO FINISH IT BEFORE YOU...

YOU WISH! I AM ON THE LAST PAGE TOO!

THEY WERE READING DETECTIVE NOVELS BY THE FAMOUS WRITER, BINOCULAR BHIDE – BB, FOR SHORT!

FINISHED!!...

YOU KNOW WHAT, AFTER READING BB'S BOOK, I'VE REALISED...

...THAT WE ARE VERY MUCH LIKE THE DETECTIVE IN HIS NOVELS!!

DETECTIVE PRATAP, YOU MEAN? I AGREE!!

CROOKS FEAR HIM...

CRIMINALS DREAD HIM...

DARK FORCES BEWARE...

FOR HERE COMES...

DETECTIVE PRATAP!!

11

13

17

Defective Detectives
Nightmare in the Museum!

Story: Sharmishta Sinha
Script: Rajani Thindiath
Art: Abhijeet Kini

RAVI'S FAMILY HAS A GUEST STAYING WITH THEM, AND ONE DAY –

AAAARGH! THE MANUSCRIPT OF THE PHARAOH WILL BE THE DEATH OF ME!

SIR?!

I FOUND A PICTURE OF SOMETHING CALLED THE 'PHARAOH'S HEART'. I THINK IT'S A SYMBOL FOR SOMETHING BUT I CAN'T FIGURE OUT WHAT! I'LL HAVE TO REFER TO THE HUNDREDS OF BOOKS IN THE DEPARTMENT LIBRARY!

WHO'S EINSTEIN?

PROFESSOR PANIGRAHI. HE WAS DAD'S PROFESSOR AT COLLEGE. HE'S NOW WITH THE DEPARTMENT OF ANTIQUITIES AT THE NATIONAL MUSEUM.

UNCLE, CAN I HELP YOU FIND THE MEANING OF THE SYMBOL? I LOVE CODES!

ERR...I GUESS I COULD GIVE YOU A PICTURE OF THE SYMBOL AND YOU COULD LOOK THROUGH THE BOOKS FOR IT...

WE'D LIKE TO HELP TOO!

AFTER ALL WE ARE THE DETECTIVES!

BUZZ OFF! I SAID IT FIRST!

SO? WE ARE THE EXPERTS!

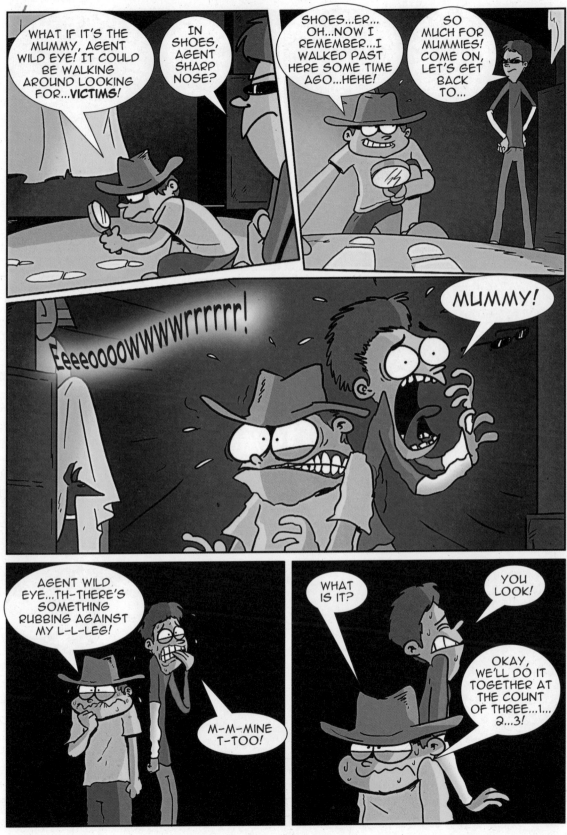

23

24

25

DEFECTIVE DETECTIVES
Mystery of the Vanishing Vegetables

Story: Ashwini Falnikar
Illustrator: Abhijeet Kini
Colourist: Umesh Sarode

28

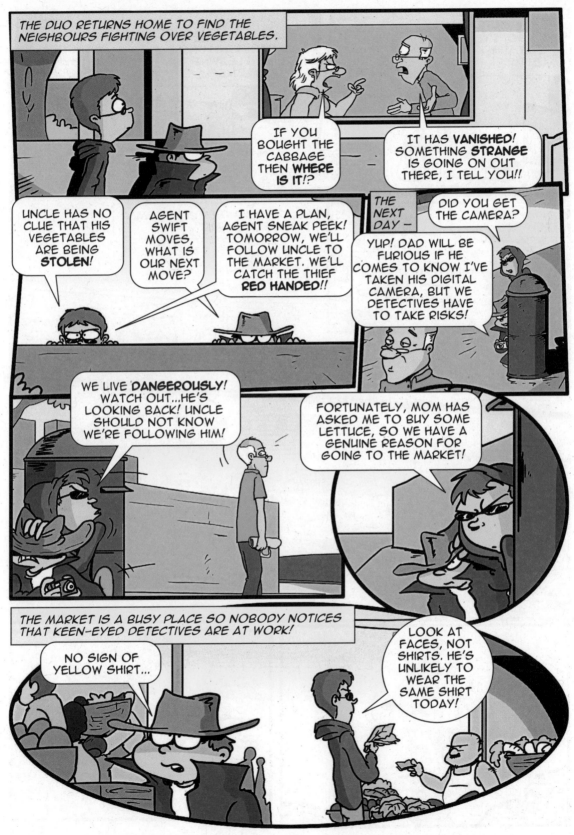

29

33

34

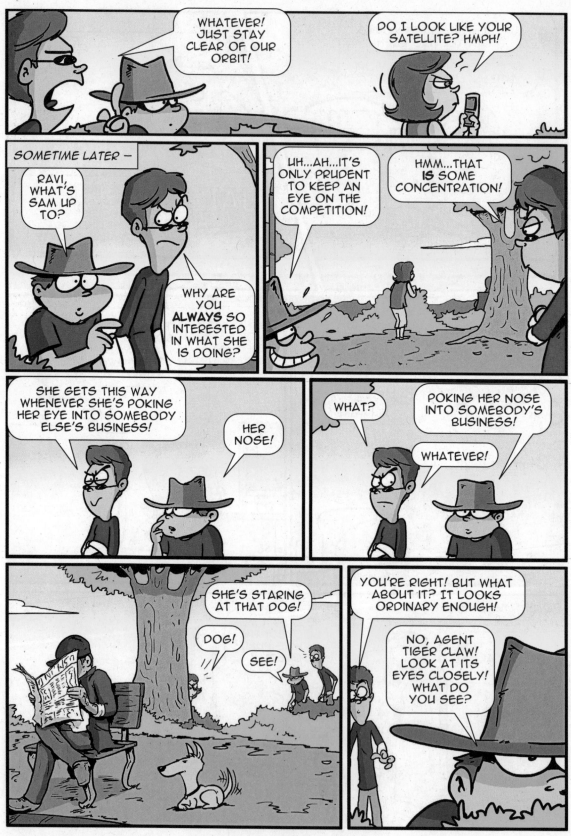

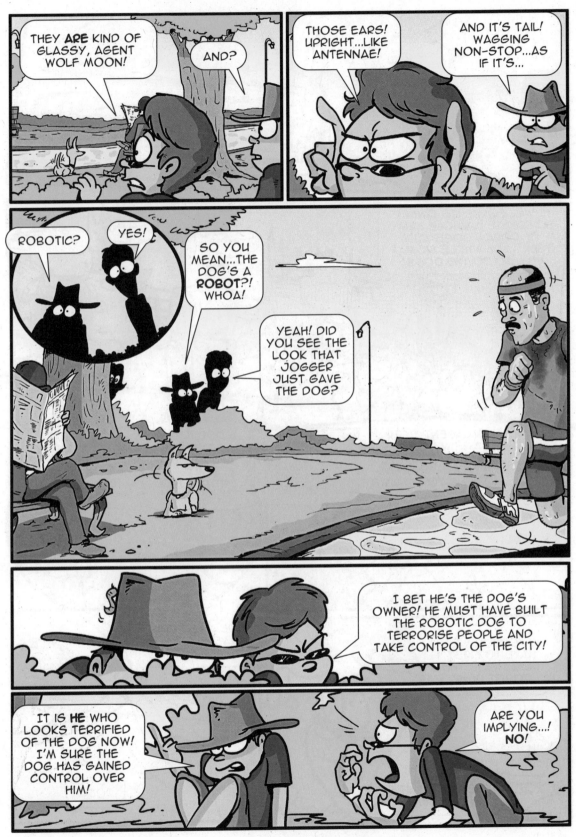

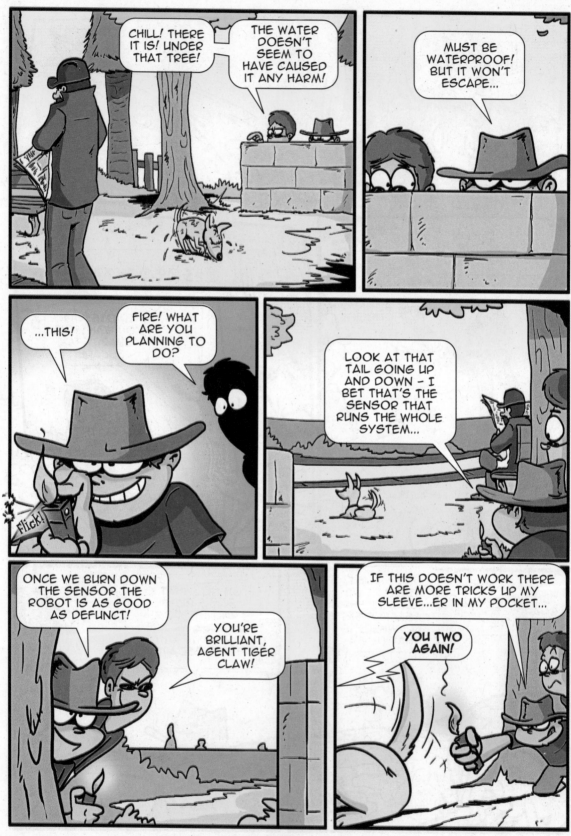

40

41

43

SUBSCRIBE NOW!

TINKLE MAGAZINE (FORTNIGHTLY)		TINKLE DOUBLE DIGEST	TINKLE COMBO TINKLE MAGAZINE (FORTNIGHTLY) + TINKLE DIGEST	
1 Year subscription	2 Year subscription	1 Year subscription	1 Year subscription	2 Year subscription
Pay only ₹720 **₹639** 24 ISSUES	Pay only ₹1440 **₹1359** 48 ISSUES	Pay only ₹1440 **₹999** 12 ISSUES	Pay only ₹1560 **₹1499** 24 ISSUES + 12 ISSUES	Pay only ₹3120 **₹2699** 48 ISSUES + 24 ISSUES

TINKLE MAGAZINE
☐ 1 YEAR | ☐ 2 YEAR

TINKLE DOUBLE DIGEST
☐ 1 YEAR

TINKLE COMBO
☐ 1 YEAR | ☐ 2 YEAR

Please tick the appropriate box(es)

YOUR DETAILS*

Name: ....

Date of birth: ☐☐ ☐☐ ☐☐☐☐

Address: ....

.... Pincode: ☐☐☐☐☐☐

School: ....

City: .... State: ....

Phone/ Mobile No.: ☐☐☐☐☐☐☐☐☐☐☐☐

Email: ....

Parent's Signature

PAYMENT OPTIONS

Cheque/DD: ☐☐☐☐☐☐

Please find enclosed cheque / DD no. .... drawn in favour of '**ACK MEDIA DIRECT LTD.**' on bank

....

for amount .... Dated: ☐☐ ☐☐ ☐☐☐☐

and send it to: ACK Media Direct Ltd. 201 & 202, Sumer Plaza, 2nd Floor, Marol Maroshi Road, Andheri (East), Mumbai 400 059.

You can subscribe online at www.amarchitrakatha.com

*Please fill all the fields to activate your subscription.

For any queries or further information:
Email: customerservice@ack-media.com | Call: 022-49188881/2/3

*T & C apply

DEFECTIVE DETECTIVES
THE PIRATE

Writer: Sharmistha Sinha
Art: Abhijeet Kini
Letterer: Pranay Bendre

ONE SUNDAY AFTERNOON, AT THE MOVIE THEATRE...

AAACHOOOO!

A LITTLE LATER...

(SNIFF!) RAVI, ARE THERE ANY PIRATES ANYMORE?

OF COURSE NOT, SILLY. THERE IS NO SUCH THING AS...

EEEEEEEKS!!!

!!!

A PIRATE! YOU SAID THERE WEREN'T ANY...

MAYBE THERE IS JUST ONE LEFT THAT NOBODY KNOWS ABOUT... LET'S FOLLOW HIM.

48

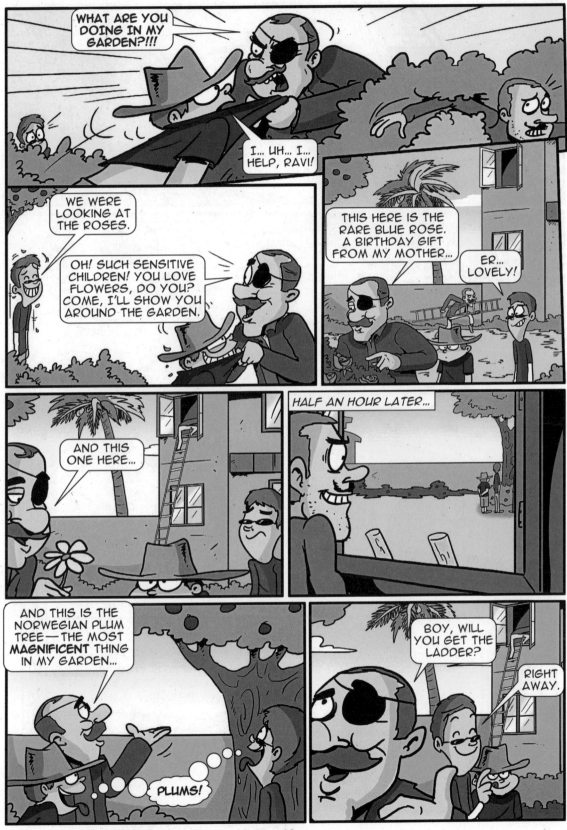

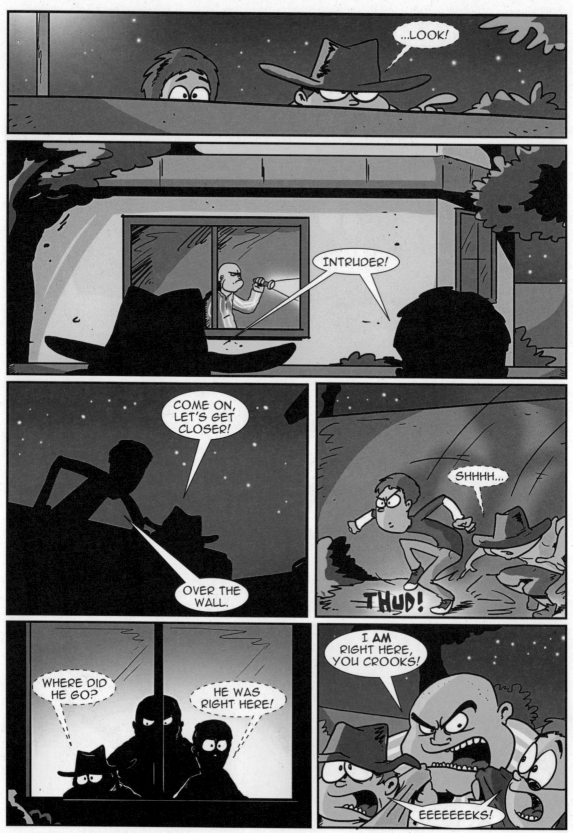

55

The Lost Civilisation

Story: Sharmistha Sinha
Art: Abhijeet Kini
Letterer: Pranay Bendre

64

65

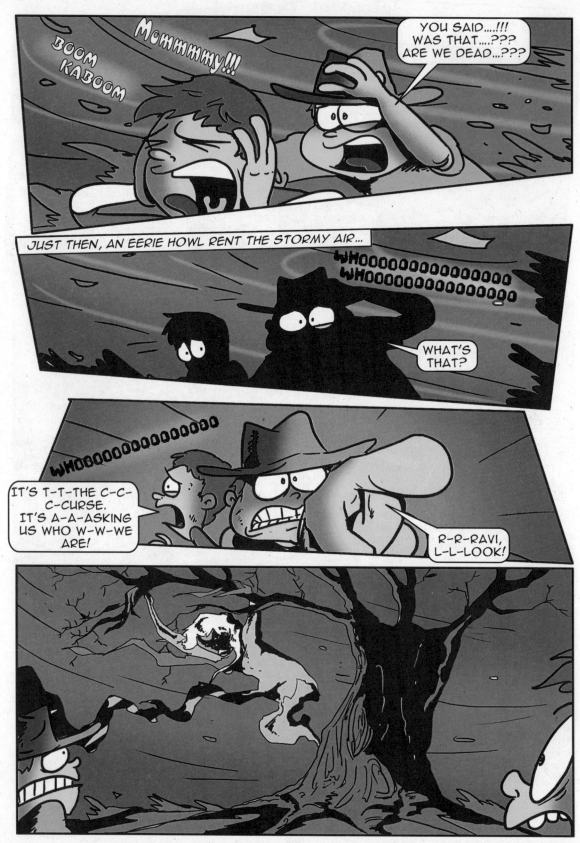

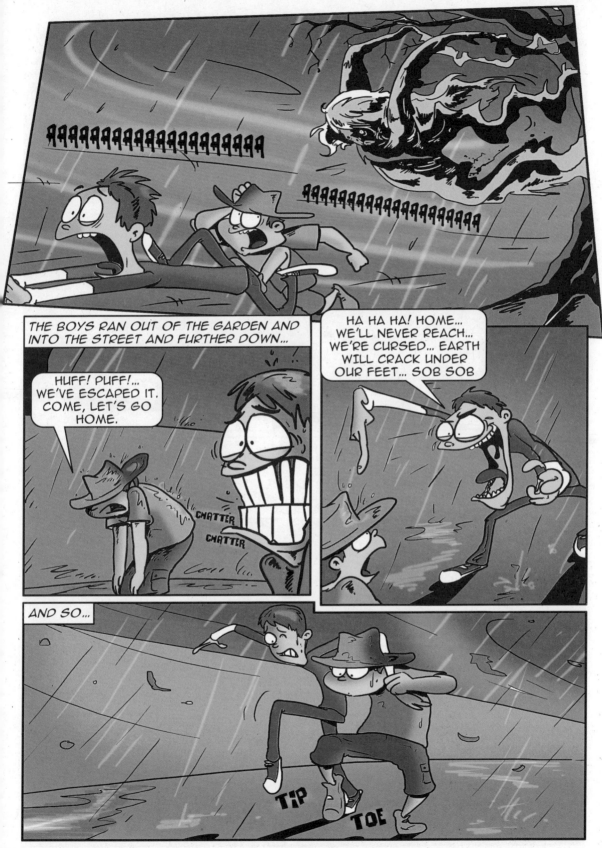

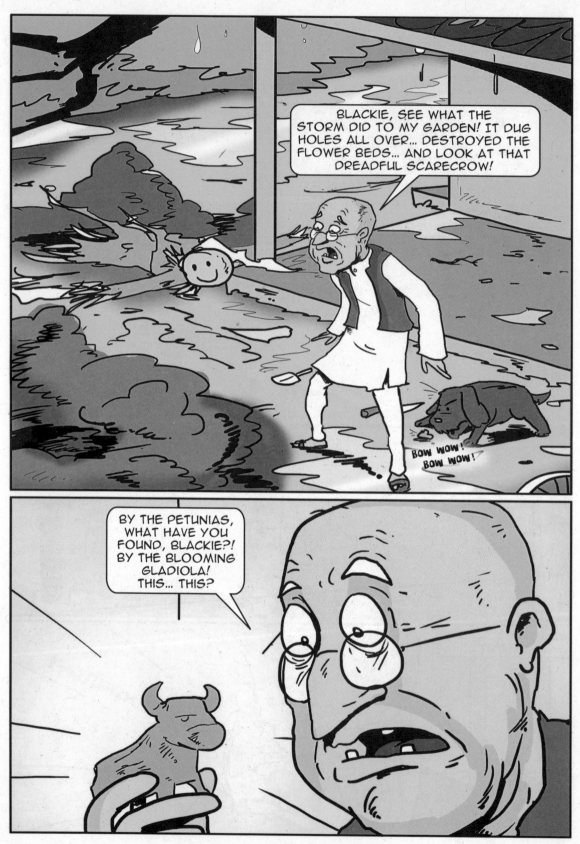